KIM THE DETEC

Cover still shows, from left
David Friedman as Specs (I

Cover still by courtesy of B … & Co., Munich.

KIM THE DETECTIVE
The first in a series

Also available:

KIM AND THE BURIED TREASURE

Jens K. Holm

Kim the Detective

Futura Publications Limited
A Contact Book

A Contact Book

First published in Great Britain in 1975
by Arthur Barker Limited
First Futura Publications edition 1975
published in association with Arthur Barker Ltd

ISBN: 0 8600 7225 8

Printed in Great Britain by
Cox & Wyman Ltd
London, Reading and Fakenham

Futura Publications Limited
110 Warner Road
London SE5

First filmed in Great Britain by Antrobus Films Ltd
as an Antrobus/Taurus co-production

A 10-part BBC television series entitled KIM & CO

Chapter 1

As the train pulled in to the little station on the north coast of Zealand, the biggest of the Danish islands, I forgot all about Katya. I leaned out of the window, forgetting that she was standing right behind me and couldn't see anything. I knew this place so well from other summer holidays; it was good to see it all again!

Nothing had changed. The station master was as short and fat as ever, standing there with his hands behind his back just the same as usual. And as usual his wife had pulled back the curtains a little and was looking out of the window. Maybe her little sandy-coloured dog was a bit fatter than last summer, but apart from that *he* was no different either. There were tufts of long grass pushing their way up between the paving-stones on the platform too, the same as last year. I was really pleased to find everything just the way I'd left it. Leaning right out of the window, I felt for the first time that the holidays were really and truly beginning.

Actually all this I'm telling you, about what I saw and what I felt, only took about a minute, and then the train stopped.

I looked for Erik. He was sure to have come to the station to meet me, but at the moment I couldn't see him. Erik and I go to the same school in Copenhagen, and we stay quite close to each other up here in the summer. We go swimming together, and dig caves together, and a lot of other things. Or rather, we did last year. Maybe we wouldn't be digging any caves this year; we might find we'd grown out of such things.

Then I remembered Katya, and I turned round, but she was gone. I got my luggage out of the rack at top speed. I'd hoped to get a proper suitcase these holidays, but that idea fell through at the last moment, so I was making do with brown paper parcels, the same as usual. I don't mind all that much, except of course a suitcase looks much smarter.

As I got out of the train I saw Erik shoot out of the station waiting room, stop, and look around him. He'd been here a week already, and by now he'd had so much sun that I hardly recognized him. His face was red as a tomato, and his hair was bleached almost white. Beside him, I felt very pale.

'Hi, Erik!' I shouted, and he turned his head and spotted me. That was all I had time for just then, because I dropped one of my parcels and it fell under the train. The station master came over to me, shouting angrily. He looked like a hippopotamus in a temper. 'Get down there, quick, and pick your stuff up!' he shouted. 'Hurry up! The train won't start till I blow the whistle.'

Erik and I jumped down and crawled under the train. The parcel had burst, scattering its entire contents among the wheels. We snatched the things up in a hurry and climbed back on the platform. Some people who had been watching were laughing at us.

Dropping my parcel made me feel all on edge. What a way to begin the holidays! But come to think of it, something like that usually did happen every time I arrived, and we always had good holidays all the same.

We fetched my bike, which had been unloaded from the guard's van by now. 'It's great to see you!' said Erik, bashing me on the back. 'It's been dead boring here this week.'

'Haven't you been swimming?'

'You bet! Every day. I went in four times yesterday. Hey, Kim, I went round to see your aunt and uncle this morning. You hungry?'

'Of course,' I said. 'Why?'

'Your aunt's got steak for lunch.'

'And cold buttermilk soup?'

Erik winked at me. 'How ever did you guess?'

Splendid! I thought. Everything was just right. For the last three years my aunt had had steak and cold buttermilk soup for lunch every time I arrived, and it was the same this year. In fact, I'd have been quite disappointed if it had been anything else for lunch, though there are a lot of other things I like to eat too.

We tied the parcels on my bike, and were just about to set off when I suddenly remembered Katya. What with seeing Erik again, and then dropping my parcel, I'd almost forgotten her for the second time. She was standing outside the waiting room, all by herself, looking rather small. She had put her case down on the gravel, and she was just standing there, waiting. I'd told her she could go with us and I'd show her the way to Moor House. How stupid of me to forget!

'Hey, Erik,' I said, 'we're taking her with us.'

'Who?'

'That girl there, with the case.'

'What for?'

'Her name's Katya.'

'So what?' said Erik. 'Do you know her?'

'Well, not exactly . . . I just met her on the train. She's going to live at Moor House, and I promised to show her the . . .'

'Moor House? You mean where that foreigner's living?'

'She lives with her father – what does he look like, then?'

'Very hairy around the face; he's got this great big beard, but it doesn't look bad, though. And he looks terribly clever and learned – yuk! And . . .'

'Hold on a moment,' I whispered, because we were quite close to Katya now, and

I didn't specially want her to hear us discussing her father.

'This is Erik,' I told her. 'Here, give us your case – I'll put it on my bike.'

'Oh, thanks,' she said. 'Are you sure it's all right?'

'Yes, of course – sorry I took a bit of a time,' I apologized. 'I dropped a parcel, and then I had to get all this stuff on the bike, see, so I . . .

'That's all right,' she said. 'Anyway, I saw you drop the parcel.'

Feeling rather annoyed that she had seen my accident, I pushed the bike out of the station yard.

The road from the station to my aunt and uncle's house is very sandy. It goes uphill for quite a way, so steeply that Erik and I had to push the bikes. Katya walked beside us. I forgot to say it was about twelve o'clock, so it was really boiling hot as we walked along the path, which has high banks on either side. We raised thick clouds of yellow dust.

Erik kept glancing rather suspiciously

at Katya. I knew he'd rather we were on our own, so we could talk properly; with Katya there, we couldn't either of us think of much to say.

Personally, I was thinking how nice it would be to have lunch and then go in the water.

Suddenly, however, Erik said, 'Hey, I nearly forgot to tell you about Specs!'

'Specs?' I said, surprised. 'What about him?'

'Well, it was like this . . . I was . . . well, I'll begin at the beginning. I was in the village shop on Monday, you see, waiting to be served, and I heard someone ask for twelve metres of electric cable. It was a boy's voice, and I thought: well, he must be crazy – what does he want twelve metres of electric cable for in the country, in summer? Then I suddenly realized I knew the voice, and when I looked, who do you think I saw?'

'Specs!' I said, drily.

'Brilliant, aren't you?' said Erik. 'Got it in one! It really was Specs, standing there large as life and twice as natural. Well, he got his electric cable and was gone again before

I could ask what he wanted it for. He's *staying* here, Kim.'

'Whereabouts?'

'In the brown bungalow down there – you know, the one with the green roof. His parents have rented it for the whole summer.'

'Why, that's right next door to Moor House,' I said.

'Anyway, we don't need to bother about him,' Erik assured me. 'If he tries butting in we can just give him the push-off.'

'Specs is funny,' I said, thoughtfully.

'Funny? He's right off his nut! Him and his inventions! He's gone and turned the empty garage into a lab. Can you understand anyone actually *wanting* to do physics and chemistry in the holidays?'

'No. At least, I wouldn't!' I said.

'Specs is a boy who goes to school with us,' I explained to Katya. 'He's mad on physics. Sometimes he asks the most peculiar questions in physics lessons – ones even the physics master can't answer, and after the physics master's been rabbiting on about it for quarter of an hour or so, Specs gets up again and answers the question himself! I mean, he might say, "I was wondering if it might be something like this, sir . . ." And then he gets a glowing report!'

'Why don't you like this Specs, then?' asked Katya.

It was the first remark she'd made since we left the station.

'Don't know,' Erik admitted.

'Well . . . I suppose he's not so bad, really,' I said. 'Just got a screw loose, that's all.'

We walked the rest of the way in silence. It was too hot to talk. Too dusty, too.

First we dropped Katya off at Moor House, and then Erik and I went on to the village. As we passed the brown bungalow, I kept an eye open for Specs, but he was nowhere to be seen. Erik went as far as my uncle's house with me, but he said he wouldn't come in, so we fixed up to go bathing at three o'clock.

Chapter 2

Perhaps I ought to tell you a bit about my aunt and uncle, because they're not just ordinary people. (Though come to think of it, not many people really *are* just ordinary.) But I don't want to write about them now; I'll come back to that later. There isn't much to say about lunch except that it was very good. My attic bedroom was the same as ever, the same pictures and all. The pictures are very ugly, really, but I like them, because I know them and I've got used to them. One of them is a photograph of a painting of two ugly, fat angels looking down from heaven. My fingers always itch to draw moustaches on them, but so far I haven't yielded to temptation. My aunt just might not like it; she seems to think well of angels.

Personally, it's beyond me how anyone *could* go and hang a thing like that on their wall. All the same, I think I'd miss them if I came out here one summer and found they'd been taken down.

At three o'clock I found my swimming trunks and picked Erik up at his place. We ran along the beach with Schnapp at our heels. Schnapp is Erik's dog; he's small and black and curly-haired, a crazy mixture of all possible breeds.

Erik often says Schnapp is cleverer than most people. Well, I don't know what kind of people Erik gets visiting his house, so I will only say that, as dogs go, Schnapp is certainly clever.

We ran about, and threw stones into the water, and Schnapp ran out to try and retrieve them, wagging his tail like mad. He is good at that, anyway.

Then we went into the water ourselves, while Schnapp lay on the beach, whining. We had a swimming race, which Erik won. However, it was my first bathe in the sea, and I told myself I'd be as fit as he was in a week's time.

When we came out we lay on the beach and sunbathed and talked, burying our fingers and toes in the warm sand. Schnapp had gone to sleep beside our clothes. And then we just lay there and dozed. I worked out that I still had sixty-nine days of holidays ahead. I tried to do some more sums and work out how many hours and then how many minutes and seconds, but finally, like Schnapp, I dropped off to sleep.

I woke to find Erik shaking me. 'Wake up, can't you?'

I sat up. 'What's the matter?'

'You were asking what Katya's father looks like. Well, that's him, over there.'

I looked across the beach. There was a man coming towards us, walking slowly, looking as if he were puzzling out some very difficult problem. He kept his eyes cast down, as if he'd lost something in the sand.

I couldn't see his face properly, but I could see the beard Erik had mentioned all right. He looked old, probably older than he was, on account of the beard; I knew Katya had been born in the same year as Erik and me.

He didn't actually pass us; he turned off into the dunes, where there is a narrow path leading to the Park.

'He's peculiar, isn't he?' said Erik.

'Yes,' I agreed. 'He does look odd. Hey, Erik, do you like Katya?'

'I suppose she's all right, so far,' said Erik grudgingly. 'But you know what girls are! They always spoil things.'

'Don't be so narrow-minded!' I told him.

There were two other men coming along the beach. When they reached the spot where Katya's father had turned off, they stopped and stood still for a moment, looking around them. We could see they were talking to each other; they seemed to be having an argument. Then they too turned off along the path, and soon they were out of sight. We thought nothing of this little incident at the time. We didn't even notice what they looked like.

Chapter 3

I think it's time I told you a bit about this place. It's a fishing village and seaside resort on the north coast of Zealand. My uncle has a villa on the outskirts of the fishing village proper. Next to our garden there's a path going down to the Kattegat, and then a field, and then the Park. On the other side of the Park you come to the seaside resort, with lots of houses and bungalows, and stalls on the sea front, and hotels. All the big shops are in this part, of course, and there are always masses of people walking around in bathing costumes or white linen suits.

The place is even busier in the evening. One or other of the hotels has a party going on almost every night in summer, with coloured lanterns hanging in the trees, and dancing till morning – I often lie awake half the night, listening to the music through my open window.

The Park isn't a real park; the name really applies only to the bit near our garden, and all the rest is more like a big wood, mainly pine trees, but some oaks and birches too.

There are large areas of this wood where almost no one ever goes. When I say 'almost no one' I mean no one but Erik and me – but we spend a lot of time there. That's where our cave was, too. We had begun digging it out last year, but we hadn't got very far. This year we went to inspect it the day after I arrived, and we both felt keen to finish the work. We decided to make it quite large and really weatherproof.

I thought it would be nice to show Katya the cave when it was ready. We'd run into her a couple of times and passed the time of day, and she had gone swimming with us once – but only once, because Erik was afraid she might come to take it for granted.

As we walked back from the wood we passed a garden where a man was hanging up lanterns. He was standing on a ladder to reach up to the trees, and having a bit of difficulty. Just as we were passing he dropped one of the lanterns, and it fell on the path on the other side of the hedge. Erik picked it up.

'Having a party?' I asked, for something to say.

'That's right. It's St John's Eve tomorrow.' We have great midsummer festivities on St John's Eve in Denmark.

'So it is!' I said. I'd quite forgotten, and so had Erik. We had no idea whether it was Thursday or Friday, or what the date was. After all, what's the point of holidays if you have to keep remembering the date?

'Well, if you look in this direction tomorrow evening, about midnight, you'll see some fireworks to remember!'

'Fireworks!' cried Erik. We're both mad about fireworks. At school last winter, we'd agreed to save up a lot of money to buy some really good fireworks for St John's Eve.

And now here we were, with one day to go, and a couple of hours earlier we'd spent the last money we had on ice cream!

We walked on in gloomy silence.

As we passed Moor House, I looked for Katya, but I couldn't see her. Instead, we ran right into Specs. He was wearing a torn blue shirt, and his hair was all tangled.

'Hi!' he shouted cheerfully.

'Hi,' we replied, a lot less cheerfully. We were not in a specially good mood.

'Like to see my lab?' he asked, pointing to the garage.

'No,' said Erik, briefly.

I gave Erik a shove. 'Sure!' I said. 'It must be very interesting.'

Well, after all, Specs *did* go to school with us, and he'd given us a lot of fun in physics lessons, not to mention saving our bacon several times when we were afraid we'd have a test, and he had asked the physics master some of his crazy questions, thus distracting his attention so that he forgot to test us at all! And it wasn't *his* fault if we were in a bad mood.

'Come on, then,' he said. 'We'll have to go in at the back.' He pointed to show us the way.

Personally, I don't know what people see in all that scientific stuff, but if you fancy that sort of thing you'd have thought it was a magnificent lab. There were retorts and test tubes and a whole crowd of glass pipes and rubber tubes on one side of the garage, and shelves groaning under the weight of what looked like lorry-loads of chemicals. On the other side of the room, there was a table with something that appeared to be the innards of a radio set on it, and there were peculiar pieces of machinery dotted about everywhere. A small board with a voltmeter and other mysterious objects had electric wires running from it in all directions.

'That's a distributor,' Specs explained.

'Crikey!' murmured Erik, quite impressed. 'You've really got something here!'

Specs explained his things to us. There was a lot we couldn't understand, but it did sound interesting. After a bit Erik said, 'Hey, Kim, we'll have to go! Time's getting on.'

Specs accompanied us to the garden gate.

'Be seeing you, Specs,' I said, as we left. 'And thanks for showing us your lab. It was really interesting.'

'Glad you liked it. Come back when I've got them ready,' he called after us.

'Sure,' said Erik vaguely.

'When you've got what ready?' I asked, puzzled.

'My rockets.'

'Rock . . . what was that you said, Specs?' Erik was back by the garden gate at the speed of light. 'Did you say *rockets*?'

Specs stared at us in surprise. 'But that's

what I was telling you about. I just showed you! Those were my rockets!'

'Yes, well, anyway!' said Erik impatiently. 'When you say rockets, do you mean *real* rockets? Ones you can fire off?'

'Of course,' said Specs simply.

'Here, let's go back inside and discuss this whole thing properly!' said Erik breathlessly, almost pushing Specs back into the garage.

Erik and I sat down, each on a packing-case, and looked at Specs standing there blinking at us. You could see what *he* was thinking: those two have a screw loose somewhere!

'If you're working on that kind of thing, could you make the firework sort of rockets too?' I asked. 'And how long would it take to make them?'

'A lot of them!' added Erik.

'Listen, if Erik and I help you, could you make some by tomorrow evening? You know it's St John's Eve tomorrow, don't you?'

'I bet he doesn't!' said Erik. 'Some people never have any idea of time.'

'Shut up, you. He can't get a word in

edgeways,' I told Erik. 'Specs, don't you think that if we all three . . .'

'Mmph . . . yes, I've got the stuff we'd need . . . OK, let's make some fireworks for tomorrow evening! Yes! Yes, this should be good!'

'You mean you *will*?'

'Of course. Why not?'

Erik had jumped up and was dancing about the place like a mad thing.

'Why not? he says. Why not? I always said it! Specs is one of the best, I said!'

'You never said any such thing!' said Specs.

'Mm, well, maybe not, but I'm saying it now, aren't I? What's more, I think I really mean it!'

'Come on, let's get moving!' I said, closing the conversation.

Chapter 4

The pile of completed firework cases in one corner of the lab was growing. We'd all been home to lunch, and now we were hard at work again. Specs was in charge; he knew a lot more about it than we did, and as he pointed out, fireworks can be dangerous if you don't understand all about them, so we were quite happy for him to be boss. We worked for some time, rolling cardboard into tubes, sticking them together and closing up one end. Erik was busy sawing long thin sticks to the right length. Suddenly he put the saw down. 'Specs,' he said eagerly, 'if we can make rockets, how about catherine wheels and bangers and so on? Could we make them too?'

'Of course. Practically anything.' Specs threw a ball of string at a fly on the wall. 'This is going to be the best firework show this place has ever seen!'

'Can we do it in the time?'

'Time *is* a problem,' Specs admitted. 'Still,

let's see what we can do . . . I know what,' he went on. 'There's a girl called Katya living over there in Moor House. She's been here once or twice, and we talked a bit. We could ask her to come and help, if you didn't mind . . .'

'Oh, you mean you know her too?' asked Erik, not exactly thrilled.

'Specs, that's a great idea!' I said. 'She could put the sticks on the rockets!' I thought Erik was going to object, so I added quickly, 'In fact, I think that may be the only way to get finished in time.'

Specs went off, leaving the door open. The sun was going down, and the trees in the Park were dark outlines against the small triangle of sea we could see through the door-way. The sun was still shining on the sea, and the water gleamed. The sail of a boat slowly drifting along was white in the sunlight.

When Specs came back, I was pleased to see he had Katya with him.

'Hullo – nice of you to ask me!' she said. 'I get a bit bored in the evening, not knowing anyone much round here.'

'Do you think you could glue these

wretched sticks to the cardboard tubes there?' asked Erik.

'I'll have a go,' said Katya.

At four-thirty on St John's Eve itself, we had finished. We had a magnificent array of rockets and Roman candles and catherine wheels and Golden Rain.

All the St John's Eves I can remember have been cold and blustery, with heavy showers of rain threatening to put the bonfires out and drive everyone indoors. But this year it was a warm, still evening, and the weather stayed fine all night. The sky was almost cloudless, and as we waited for it to get properly dark we felt the sun would never set.

Down on the beach, a huge bonfire had been built, and quite early in the evening, long before it was due to be lit, people were gathering around, standing about in groups and chatting, or wandering up and down the beach.

Katya would have to stay with her father; he didn't like being on his own among such a crowd, because he didn't speak Danish too well. Erik, Specs and I had divided out the fireworks between us. We each had a hiding place in the dunes: one right behind the bonfire, one a bit to the south of it, and one a little further north. We hadn't breathed a word to anyone, so it would be a big surprise. I was stationed right beside the path, and I had made myself a sort of shelter among the bushes (horribly prickly they were, too), so that even if people passed quite close they wouldn't guess there was anyone there.

We left the fireworks at our hiding places and strolled around in the crowd with Schnapp, waiting for things to start. At last the sun sank below the horizon. There was a sailing boat coming slowly in from the Sound. Its crew were singing and waving lighted torches.

We watched the boat until it disappeared beyond the promontory. When it was out of sight, you suddenly noticed how dark it was.

The man who kept the village shop poured a whole tin of paraffin over the bonfire, and someone threw a burning match on it. The flames leaped up at once, and the bonfire burned bright and clear, with hardly any smoke.

Then we all sang songs. The fire crackled

and hissed, and as it became hotter the circle of onlookers around it spread out. We saw Katya and her father and said hullo to them. They were standing with their backs to the water. Katya was joining in the singing, while her father just stood there looking at the flames.

Somebody bashed me on the back. Specs.

'We're going now.'

I pushed my way out of the circle.

'The bonfire's nearly burnt down. When it's right out we'll start the fireworks.'

'Who's going to begin?'

'Why don't we let Erik go first?' I suggested. 'With a rocket right across the bonfire!'

'Yes, that'll be our signal.'

'Right,' Erik agreed. 'As soon as mine goes up, you two begin. This is going to be great!'

We parted and went off to our separate hiding places. I felt in my pocket to make sure I hadn't forgotten the matches, sat down and waited. Down on the beach they'd started another song.

Someone was coming along the narrow path towards me. Two men: I could hear from their footsteps. I sat perfectly still. They stopped. I held my breath. My arm was pressed right against a thorny branch, but I dared not take it away for fear of making a noise. I lay there motionless, wishing they would walk on. Then I heard one of them say:

'Down there – that's him. With the girl.'

'Yes, you can hardly miss him, can you, with that beard?'

'Better not go too close. He might see us.'

They left the path and went further away from me, their voices growing fainter and fainter, and though I strained my ears I couldn't hear any more.

When Erik let off his first rocket, I was so startled I dropped the matches. Luckily I found them again quite quickly, and next minute my own first rocket was whizzing through the air. Specs soon got going too. It looked fantastic.

When at last all the rockets and Roman candles and Golden Rains were out, we finished the show with some loud bangers.

Everyone applauded, and when we came back to the bonfire someone gave us three cheers, and people crowded up to thank us for the show. We enjoyed being the centre of attention.

When I finally got to bed, late that night, I remembered the two men. I'd quite forgotten them in the excitement of the fireworks. I tried to remember what I'd caught of their conversation, but I couldn't call much of it to mind. What could it have been about? I decided to tell Katya about it next time I saw her. Or perhaps not . . . why alarm her? Then my thoughts all got muddled up, and I fell asleep. I was really tired. It had been a marvellous day.

Chapter 5

Next day, I was lying on the ground in the wood near our cave, waiting for the others. We'd agreed to meet here and put in some work on the cave, so as to get it finished soon.

The weather was still fine. The sun was shining through the leaves, the birds were singing, in fact everything was lovely. I lay there dozing, with my hands clasped behind my neck.

'Hullo!' Erik pushed his way energetically through the undergrowth. I'd half heard him coming for some time, without really taking much notice.

'Hi.'

'Others not here yet?'

'No.'

'You look terribly lazy.'

'I *am* terribly lazy.'

'I thought we were going to get a lot of work done.'

'Not me! I've decided not to do a stroke

of work today! I intend to lie here and watch the rest of you.'

'That's what *you* think! Brought the axe?'

I nodded.

'And here's the saw. But we can wait till the others come. Want a cigarette?'

'Sure!' I said. 'Where did you get them?'

'Pinched them from home.'

'Shouldn't we wait for the others?'

'I've got a whole packet – here you are.'

'Thanks.'

Erik lay down on the grass beside me.

'Got a light?'

'Here.'

We lit our cigarettes and lay there smoking in silence for some time. An ant ran over the moss. I blew smoke at it to try and make it cough, but it wasn't playing; it just ran off in a fright. The grey smoke clung around the damp moss.

'Ah, that's good!' said Erik fervently.

'Yes,' I agreed, 'just what I needed.'

'How right you are!'

'A cigarette tastes really great!'

Erik looked sideways at me. I pretended not to notice, and studied the sky attentively.

It was deep blue, with big white clouds.

'Kim, do you *honestly* think so?'

'Er . . . no!' I said, truthfully.

'Then why did you say so?'

'Oh, I don't know. Perhaps I thought it *did* taste great when I said that.'

'But that was only two seconds ago!'

'Well, a person can change his mind, can't he?' I said airily.

'Not in two seconds flat! If you ask me, we're a couple of nut cases!'

'Why?'

'Lying here smoking, when there's no one to see us but ourselves.'

'I thought you were smoking because you liked it?'

'I hate it!' said Erik. 'But it kind of *looks* good.'

I stubbed my cigarette out on a stone.

'Well, then, no point in smoking when we're on our own.'

'Dead right!' said Erik, relieved. 'Let's keep it till the others turn up.'

'Good idea.'

'Shall we start on the cave?'

We began work. First we cleared the dead leaves and twigs out of the cave.

'You know, it wouldn't be a bad idea to pull the whole lot down.'

'Think so!'

'Yes – it's going to be too small anyway, now there are four of us. If we pull the front part right away, and enlarge the cave inside, and then start again, making the whole thing bigger . . .'

'Mmph. We could cut down some branches with the axe.'

'And make a proper floor.'

'We could make it a real log cabin, like in Westerns.'

'Great! The idea of the century!'

We set to work at once. First we pulled down all the structure we'd built last year. We realized now that we hadn't really built it very well. We sorted out those twigs and branches that were still any use and put them on one side, and made a pile of the rest outside the cave.

'We can use them for a camp fire.'

'Yes – when it's all finished, we'll have a party!'

'Terrific! Let's do that.'

We worked hard for a long time. When Specs and Katya finally turned up, we had cleared a big space where we were going to build our log cabin.

Specs had brought another axe and saw, and a whole rucksack full of nails and pincers and other tools. Katya was carrying a basket, but it was covered and I couldn't see what was inside.

'We had quite a job finding you,' she said. 'We've been all over the place, trying to track you down by your voices. You're not usually this quiet!'

'Believe it or not, we've been working!' said Erik.

'Where's the cave?'

'Well, we decided we don't need a cave any more. Listen, this is what we thought we'd do . . .'

Erik and I kept interrupting each other as we described our plan. Specs thought it was a good idea too.

'Look, will you three promise me something?' asked Katya.

'What?'

'I don't want you to treat me differently because I'm a girl – just give me some work to do! I may not be much good with an axe yet, but I'll soon learn!'

Erik tossed the bigger axe towards her.

'Fine!' he said cheerfully. 'Just start cutting that one down, will you?' And he pointed to an enormous old oak standing at the edge of the clearing.

Katya grinned back at him. 'And when it's down, what next?'

'Then you can chop it up into matchsticks!'

After a bit of discussion, we divided up the work. Specs and I collected stones for the foundations, while Katya and Erik trimmed twigs off the branches we'd already got together.

Specs and I pushed and dragged our stones across the clearing and made a heap of them. The sun was high in the sky, and there were almost no shadows. We were dripping with sweat. I'd told my aunt I wouldn't be home to lunch; I hadn't known at the time how hungry I was going to be.

'How about a little rest?' That was Erik calling after us as we went in search of more stones. We turned immediately and threw ourselves full length on the grass.

'Oof! Talk about hard work!'

'I could eat an ox!'

'Oh, shut up, will you?' said Erik crossly.

'If anyone even mentions eating, I'm liable to go stark staring mad!'

'Well, I *am* glad you're hungry!' said Katya, with a secret sort of smile. 'Hand me that basket, someone!'

We stared at her.

'You mean to say . . . ?'

'Do you like lamb chops?'

'Do we – do we *like* lamb chops!'

'Hey, not so fast! I'm just spreading out the cloth.'

'Katya,' I said solemnly, 'you have saved my life! Half an hour more and I'd have been dead of starvation! I'll do as much for you some day – at least, I hope so!'

'Don't bother, but thanks all the same!' she laughed. 'Right, let's see: there's a cold lamb chop each, and here's some bread and some tomatoes, and I brought a tin of tuna too. And four bottles of shandy. I hope it's still cold.'

'Katya,' said Erik, rolling his eyes heavenward, 'you are without a shadow of doubt the most beautiful girl I ever set eyes on in my life! You're . . . you're . . .'

'Cut it out!' said Katya drily. 'Don't just sit there, do something – like opening the tuna! Specs can deal with the shandy.'

After the meal Erik and I lit our cigarettes again; we gave Specs one too, but Katya said no. We lay full length in the grass, talking and making plans for our splendid log cabin. When we stood up and went back to work the clearing was half in shadow.

We worked all afternoon, and when we finally called it a day and tidied up our tools we'd made good progress, and we felt very pleased with ourselves.

On the way back Specs and Eric went on ahead, while Katya and I lagged behind. We didn't have to be home at any particular time, so we strolled slowly along, talking, and soon we had fallen some way behind the others.

I decided to take the bull by the horns.

'Listen, Katya – I heard someone talking about your father on St John's Eve.'

Katya turned her head quickly. 'Who?'

'Two men. I didn't know them. They were on the path, near where I was hiding with my fireworks.'

'What did they say?'

'Well, nothing much, really. I only heard a few words. I know they were discussing him, though.'

'But Father knows hardly anyone here. He doesn't speak very good Danish, you see. We – we live a very quiet life.'

'Is your father anything to do with politics?'

'No. He was a college professor, and he invented something – that's really all I know myself.'

'But if someone . . . I mean, look, are you sure he's safe here?'

'Why wouldn't he be safe? What are you getting at? Secret agent and so on?'

'Oh, well, I don't expect it means anything at all. Don't worry about it, Katya. I've probably been reading too many crime stories,' I said, hoping to calm her down.

'Kim, do you think those men . . .?'

'No, of course I don't! Tell your father if you like – I expect he'll just laugh. No, it was simply that I thought . . .'

'What did you think?'

'Well, I thought the one person who'd really know what it was about would be your father. He's the best person to judge if someone is . . . well, plotting something against him. And then he can drop a word to the police.'

'No! No . . . that's just what he can't do.'

'But why not?'

Katya's eyes were downcast. I guessed she was wondering what and how much she could tell me. I said nothing; I didn't want to press her. She had to decide for herself how far to let me into her confidence.

She stopped walking suddenly, and said, 'You see, Father can't go to the police because . . . because he hasn't got official permission to be here in Denmark! He doesn't have a passport, or any other papers.'

'But can't he *get* official permission?'

'I don't know. Perhaps. But he doesn't dare to apply.'

'Whyever not?'

'He got into this country illegally. He had to slip past the Customs and the police at the border. He might be put in prison!' She was near tears.

'Are you very fond of him?' I asked.

'Yes, very!' she said, in a muffled voice.

We walked on. 'Aren't you afraid I might tell someone?' I asked.

'No,' she said quietly, 'or else I wouldn't have told you.'

We had reached her garden gate by now, and I handed her the basket, which I'd been carrying.

'See you in the wood tomorrow!' I said. 'The others are coming too.'

'Fine!' she said, more cheerfully. 'I'll be there.'

'Good night.'

'Good night.'

I waited till the door of the house had closed behind her, and then I went home. The holidays had only just begun, but it suddenly struck me what a lot of things had happened already.

Chapter 6

After St John's Eve we had a spell of fine, dry weather. Of course the sun didn't shine all the time, but we kept quite warm enough by working on our hut. We'd each taken to bringing our own provisions, and we were always very hungry when it was time to unpack the picnic. We took our swimming things to the wood with us, too, and when we got too hot we'd drop everything and go down to the beach for a dip. Then, after swimming around for a bit, we'd go back to the wood and carry on working.

That evening we finished the hut it began to rain. We'd brought a lot of delicious things to eat, so as to celebrate, and Erik had brought his banjo, because Katya had asked him to play and sing to us as we sat round our camp fire. Personally, I hadn't asked him to do any such thing. First, because I knew what it would sound like, and second because I knew he didn't need asking. He liked the sound of his own voice so much, he'd seize the slightest excuse to burst into song!

When it began to rain, we had to put the camp fire outside our hut out, but we had a fireplace made of big stones inside the hut, so we lit a fire there. Luckily we'd collected enough wood for kindling, and the bigger bits caught easily. The smoke rose straight up through the hole we had left for it.

It rained hard, and we felt very comfortable sitting warm and dry in the middle of the wood and listening to the rain falling outside. A few drops did come in through the hole in the roof, of course, but mostly they fell into the fire.

So there we sat around our fire, gazing at the flames. The kettle began to boil, and Katya unpacked biscuits, jam, cake and tea. Specs turned to Eric.

'Going to give us a tune, then?'

Erik, who was holding his banjo on his lap and stroking it, cast me a wary glance.

'Tea first!' he said.

'You know,' said Katya, as she passed round enamel mugs of tea, 'I'm almost sorry we've finished the hut. It was hard work, building it, but I really enjoyed coming up here to do it.'

'You're nuts!' said Erik. 'I'm only too glad it's done. I've had quite enough hard work for one holiday!'

'No, I know what Katya means,' said Specs. 'Now the hut is finished we don't have anything else to *do*. Nothing to aim for! Nothing to feel pleased about, nothing to talk and dream about, nothing . . .'

'Oh, shut up, for heaven's sake!' I interrupted. 'Let's just be glad we've finished it! It's bound to come in useful some day. Tell you what – do you think we could get permission to sleep here now and then?'

'Good idea!' cried Erik.

'I know I couldn't,' said Katya sadly.

'Well, you're a girl.'

'I can't help that, can I?'

'Oh, I thought you could!' Erik teased her. 'Well, maybe Specs could fix up a telephone between here and your house. Then Auntie Katya can tell us a bedtime story before we go to sleep!'

'If you think that's funny . . .' began Katya wrathfully.

'Oh, don't argue!' I tried to make peace. 'You know, there's something in what Katya said. It's nice to have a hut of our own, of course, but we'd soon get bored sitting around drinking tea here.'

'You're right,' admitted Erik. 'You know what? We need a few enemies!'

'What do you mean, enemies?'

'You heard me! Enemies. The sort that come creeping up behind you and shoot you with poisoned arrows and . . . and all that. Like in books.'

We stared at him, eyebrows raised.

'Oh, for goodness' sake! Smugglers or gunmen or spies! You're always reading about that sort of person.'

'Well, sure, but you don't get them in real life,' I said witheringly.

But just as I said that, I remembered those two mysterious men, and my thoughts went wandering off. Then I smiled at myself. I was as bad as Eric, imagining things! I must have been reading too many crime stories too!

I brought my train of thought to a close. 'No,' I said. 'Things like that never really happen.'

'Pity, though!' said Specs. 'Oh, well, pass the jam.'

After tea Erik began to sing and play his

banjo. I will say, it didn't sound so bad, especially when he was accompanying his own singing, because then you didn't hear his voice so much.

Afterwards we talked for a bit, and listened to the rain pattering down on the roof. All of a sudden, Specs sat bolt upright.

'Erik, you're a genius!'

'Yes, I know,' said Erik modestly. 'When they hear me singing, people always say I'm . . .'

'No, I didn't mean that! Though I must admit I never heard anything like it in my life . . . I was thinking of what you said just now.'

'Oh, did I go and say something brilliant, then?'

'Yes, you did!'

'Er . . . what was it, exactly?'

'You gave me a fantastic idea!'

'Go on!'

'No, I'm keeping it a secret for the moment. But you can come to my lab tomorrow if you like, and help with something very exciting.'

We tried to get him to tell us more, but he was silent as the grave.

The fire was almost out, and the rain outside had slackened off a bit. Out in the wood a bird cried. We sat there in silence, listening to Erik strumming gently on his banjo. After a bit he began to sing:

'Come and sit by my side if you love me,
Do not hasten to bid me adieu,
But remember the Red River Valley,
And the gal that has loved you so true.'

Chapter 7

Next morning a telegram came for my uncle while we were having breakfast. He took it and opened it very deliberately. My aunt, who is rather small, was craning her neck trying to read it.

'What does it say, Carlo?'

'What an impatient girl you are!' my uncle teased her. 'Let me have a look at it first!' When he had read it, he folded it up and put it carefully in his pocket. He liked to tease her.

'Oh, come on, what does it say?'

'It says . . . it says we're having a visitor.'

'A visitor? Who?'

'Don't worry, it's only Otto Rasmussen. He's arriving on the 11.52.'

'Oh, you men! You're impossible! Why couldn't he have let us know earlier? Fancy waiting to send a telegram on the very morning he's coming! How am I supposed to get everything ready?'

'Who is this Otto Rasmussen?' I asked curiously.

'He's a publisher – he's in the firm that brought out my little book on spiders. A very nice fellow – easy to get on with. I'm sure you'll like him. We'll have some interesting conversations!'

I wasn't so sure about that. I've tried reading my uncle's little book on spiders (I should explain that spiders are his hobby). I *have* been known to read more thrilling works of literature. So it wasn't really surprising that I felt my uncle's guest would be like my uncle's book: rather dry and boring and miles away from ordinary life. Oh well, we'd see.

'You could go to the station and meet him, Kim,' my aunt suggested. 'Help him with his luggage. How long will he be staying, Carlo?'

'Oh, a week or so, I should think,' my uncle guessed. 'Mind you get to the station on time, Kim. He's never been here before. You'll recognise him quite easily – he's tall, with dark hair and strong glasses.'

'Don't worry, I'll find him', I assured my uncle.

After breakfast my aunt sent me down to the village shop, and to the butcher, and after that there were some odd jobs I'd promised to do in the garden, and so time flew by. I had to hurry so as not to be late for our meeting in the lab at eleven o'clock.

I was the last to arrive. Erik and Katya were standing around, waiting, while Specs was busy with a complicated piece of apparatus on the table.

'Hullo,' I said. 'Come on, then, Specs, what's the big idea?'

'He hasn't told us yet,' said Katya.

'I wanted to wait till you were all here. Find yourselves somewhere to sit.'

We sat down on the packing-cases and the table, as we all looked at Specs.

'Right, then,' he began. 'What Erik said yesterday gave me an idea – but I'm not really sure what you'll think of it . . .'

'The suspense is killing me!' groaned Erik.

'You see, you said something about a telephone, and I . . .'

'Oh, that!' Erik interrupted. 'Telephone – well, that was only a joke. You'd need a whole lot of wires, and goodness knows what else . . .'

'Shut up, can't you?' I told him. 'Let Specs finish!'

'Thanks!' said Specs. 'Naturally I can't fix up a telephone between here and our hut, but there are other ways of doing it.'

'Such as?' asked Katya.

'Well, like telegraphy.'

'You need wires and things for telegraphy too,' I said.

'Not for wireless telegraphy, you don't. I've been knocking something of that kind together this morning. Of course, it's very primitive. They used this sort of thing before proper radio was invented. But I've got most of the parts we'd need.'

He went over to the table and showed us a small, grubby wooden box, about the size of two matchboxes put together.

'This is an inductor,' he explained. 'They used to have these in old Ford cars, and I know a man in the garage who gave me this one.'

'Go on!' Erik urged him.

'OK, so I pass a current through it. Now, watch this . . .'

He brought two wires close together till

they were almost touching, and a lot of little blue sparks crackled between the ends of the wires.

'Crikey! That's brilliant!' said Erik, much impressed.

'All we need now is an earth, and an aerial, and a capacitor, and of course a sending key, and then we've got it!'

'You mean we could sit out in the hut and send messages back to someone here?'

'That's right,' said Specs. 'And vice versa too, of course, because I've got stuff to make two sets. I only need a few more parts for the receivers.'

'Amazing!' I murmured.

'You take my breath away,' said Erik.

Specs beamed, enjoying our admiration. 'I thought you'd like it. Now we have to get the parts we still need, and then we can start right away.'

'What'll it cost?'

'Er – well, that's the snag. I've worked it out, and I make it something like twenty-five *kroner*.'

Erik gave a long whistle.

'That's a lot of money.'

'No, it'll be all right,' Specs said. 'After

all, there are four of us – surely we can each manage to earn five or six *kroner* somehow?'

'Yes, but how?'

'Let's think . . .'

'*Palle!*' someone shouted from the house. Specs's mother. His real name is Palle, but he seems to like being called Specs better, and why not?

'Palle! Lunch is ready!'

Specs opened the door and shouted back that he was coming. 'Let's meet at the hut after supper this evening,' he said. 'Then we can pool our ideas. That gives us a whole afternoon to think of something.'

I said a hasty goodbye and dashed off to the station.

The train had already come in. I found Mr Rasmussen at once; he was standing on the platform, looking a little lost and fearfully learned. When I went up to him and introduced myself, he brightened up.

'Good of you to come and meet me!' he said warmly. 'You're Kim, aren't you? Your uncle's told me a lot about you. How hot it is today! I rather think I'm too warmly dressed!'

I had to agree with him. He was wearing a

waistcoat as well as a jacket, both black, and carrying a dark overcoat.

'It's going to be hotter than this,' I told him. 'The road to the village is right out of the wind. Maybe you should take your jacket off. I'll carry your case.'

We had quite an interesting conversation on the way home. He really did seem nice enough, though a bit dry, as I'd expected.

When we got in we were both very hungry and thirsty, so it was a good thing that lunch was ready.

Chapter 8

Directly after lunch I made my getaway and went over to Erik's house. His father was sitting out on their open veranda, smoking a cigar.

'Hullo there!' he called, when he saw me coming. 'Don't say you've come to mow our lawn!'

'No, I wasn't going to!' I said, surprised. 'Does it need mowing, then?'

'It does not. I mowed it myself only yesterday evening. However, something funny has come over Erik, and I wondered if it was catching.'

'What kind of something? Is he keen to mow lawns all of a sudden?'

'Right first time, Kim. It gave me quite a turn, I can tell you. He *offered* just now – of his own accord. Didn't I think it would be a good idea if he mowed the lawn for me? I've never known such a thing happen before, not in all the years I've known Erik!'

'Was that all he said?'

'Oh, by no means! When I said no, he wanted to paint the garden gate and creosote the roof of the shed.'

I couldn't help laughing.

'Didn't he mention money?'

'Aha! That's more like it! Well, at least you're honest, I'll say that for you. What does he want the money for?'

I told Erik's father all about it. He is the sort of person you can tell things to.

'Sounds exciting,' he said. 'Well, well! Wireless telegraphy! I must say, I quite envy you. Don't you need a licence or some such thing, though? Are you sure you're not breaking the law?'

'I don't really know . . .'

'Well, that's something you'll have to find out for yourselves. I'm not paying anyone's fine, is that quite clear? And how are you planning to get the money for the parts?'

'Er . . . ' I said, clearing my throat. 'Well, er, mowing lawns and creosoting roofs and painting gates and so on.'

'But not at this house!' said Erik's father, with a grin. 'Can't you think of anything better than that? Surely you can devise some means of making money without soaking your poor old parents! Why, when I was your age . . .'

'Yes, we'll think of something,' I interrupted hastily.

'You do that! I hope you make a success of all this, but I'm not so sure.'

'Like to bet on it?' I suggested.

'Bet! You've got a nerve, young Kim! Do you think I'd enter into a bet with you . . . on what exactly, anyway?'

'On . . . on Erik and me . . . let's say on us earning fifteen *kroner* between us by supper time today!'

'You intrigue me, I must say! How are you going to do it?'

'No idea, but we're sure to think of something.'

'Yes, you really do intrigue me!' he repeated. 'All right. If you can come back here with fifteen *kroner* by seven o'clock, I'll give you another fifteen.'

'Oh, great! Er . . . suppose we lose the bet?'

'Well, let's see . . . if you lose, you can paint the gate and creosote the fence and the shed roof free! All right?'

'Done!' I said.

'Good. Well, you'd better make a start, then. You'll find Erik in the kitchen with my wife.'

Soon afterwards, Erik and I were walking along the road, kicking up the dust with the toes of our shoes. I'd told Erik about my conversation with his father, and he was far from enthusiastic.

'What a stupid arrangement!' he grumbled. 'We may well find ourselves creosoting and painting all next week! You needn't think he'll let us wriggle out of it!'

'Who says we're going to lose the bet?'

'I do! How on earth are we supposed to earn fifteen *kroner*? The only thing I can think of just now is a bank robbery!'

'The banks are closed today.'

'There you are, see? Our last chance gone! No, my Dad knows what he's doing, all right. He's a real businessman, my Dad. He'd even make money out of a couple of poor schoolboys on holiday. We might as well start creosoting right away.'

'Don't be so spineless,' I told him. 'There must be *some* way. Let's see – who do we know around here?'

'There's old Stoffer at the garage.'

'That's it!' I cried in excitement. 'The money's as good as ours already! Don't you remember last summer – how all the drivers wanted their cars washed when they filled up?'

'Come on!' cried Erik breathlessly. 'Kim, you're a genius!'

'I know,' I agreed smugly.

Chapter 9

We found old Stoffer (his real name was Mr Christoffersen) in the darkest corner of his garage, sitting on a packing-case eating his lunchtime sandwiches.

'Hullo there, you two!' he greeted us. 'I thought you'd forgotten me this year!'

'Elephants never forget,' said Erik. 'How's your rheumatism?'

'Good heavens, boy, you make me sound like an old man! Rheumatism! Hah! I'm as chirpy as a cricket!' He stood up, with some difficulty, and limped over to his work-bench. Evidently his rheumatism wasn't as good as he'd like us to think.

I explained our bet to Stoffer, and things worked out just the way I wanted. When I'd finished, he grunted, 'Money, eh? Ah, yes, he respects money, he does! So he doesn't think you two can earn fifteen *kroner* in an afternoon, is that it? Why, of course you can! I dare say your Dad thinks the stock market is the only place a person can make money! Well, he's wrong there!' Stoffer looked scornful. We had given him all the facts; now we only had to wait while he hummed and ha'ed about it. We heard a car hoot outside. The old man opened the door, letting the sun shine in, and went out to the car. I got up to follow him, but Erik held me back.

'Better leave it to him, don't you think?'

In a few moments Stoffer came back.

'Right, off you go!' he said, grinning. 'Gentleman outside wants his car washed. Mind you do a good job!'

We were delighted. We fetched the hose and gave the car a good wash down (and ourselves too in the process). We rubbed and wiped and polished till the bodywork shone like glass. Now and then Stoffer came over to inspect our work, and nodded knowledgeably.

'Good as new!' he said approvingly, and went back inside his dark cavern again.

I'm not sure just how old Stoffer is, but he was alive when cars were first invented, and he knows about all there is to know about them. Cars are not just machines to him. 'You have to treat a car kindly,' he claimed. 'They're like children, they won't thrive without love!' And then he would look affectionately at the car in question and stroke its radiator. When he was young he raced cars, and if he feels in the mood he can tell very exciting stories about this period of his life, and the racing cars he drove.

Now, however, all he could do was limp around his little garage, repairing cars and cherishing his memories.

We'd hardly finished the first car before Stoffer had another customer for us. Giving a car a really good wash took us some time, because we were taking a lot of trouble, and we weren't very experienced.

We spent the whole afternoon washing cars, enjoying ourselves a lot. About five-thirty, when we'd washed three cars, we stopped for a rest, and sat down with Stoffer on a seat in the sun, leaning back against the warm wooden wall of the garage.

'I was going to ask you,' began Stoffer. 'That lad you call Specs – isn't he Palle Birk, from the bungalow over there?'

'That's right. Do you know him? He's in out class at school.'

'He's got a real head on his shoulders, that boy! I hope you realize that!'

'He always comes top in things like physics at school,' I agreed.

'He's all right, too,' Erik added. 'Actually, he isn't all that brilliant at school except for physics and chemistry.'

'Well, there've been a lot of great men who weren't particularly brilliant at school,' said Stoffer in a philosophical tone.

'Dead right!' said Erik and I, in chorus. 'That gives us both a chance yet!'

'Oh, laughing at me, are you?' inquired Stoffer, hurt. 'You wait, my boys! You wait and see.'

'What do you mean?'

'Didn't he tell you about the carburettor he's invented?'

'What carburettor?' I asked.

'Ah, well – this lad Palle, he set to work, and lo and behold, he's invented a brand-new type of carburettor. A new method, see? I helped him a bit with the technical side of things, but the idea is his – all his own! And a good one too, if you ask me.'

'He never breathed a word to us,' muttered Erik.

'Couldn't he sell the idea to someone?' I asked.

'Yes, he could – unless someone else gets in first with the same idea. And just now he needs money, quite a lot of money, to get it all worked out properly, and he hasn't got that kind of money. I reckon his parents aren't too well off.'

'No; they can't really afford to go away for a summer holiday, only his mother's ill – at least, she *was* ill – and the doctor said she had to have sea air.'

'I'll tell you something in confidence,' said Stoffer, lowering his voice. 'Mind you don't tell anyone else, now! We've decided to try building this carburettor of his into an old car, to see how it works in practice. But there's a lot of technical details to be tested before we get to that point – that's where we need the money, and we don't have money for that. I've got a bit of my own put by, of course, and I wouldn't mind helping, but to tell you the truth, I never set a lot of store by money, so I haven't got much in the way of savings.'

'When are you going to start?'

'Ah, well, I don't really know. It woud be best to save up enough money to get the job finished, before we make a start. That'll mean a year, most likely, before we can begin.'

'Listen, there's a car coming!' We jumped up.

The clock was striking seven as we dashed breathlessly into the Holms' living-room. Mr Holm, who had raised his eyebrows as we burst in, looked pleased when he saw his son's beaming face, and the fifteen *kroner* Erik was showing him.

'Good work!' he said approvingly. 'How did you do it?'

'Oh, it was dead easy!' said Erik, with a grand gesture.

'Well, I must say I'm delighted! I'd better admit defeat. I suppose you expect an apology?'

'Not much!' said Erik, who knew his father.

'Tell me how you earned the money.'

'Washing cars.'

'Good Lord . . . when was it I last asked you to wash *my* car, eh, Erik?'

'No idea, Dad, honestly.' Erik's face was innocent as the face of the angel on my bedroom wall.

'If you think I'm swallowing that one . . .

well, never mind! Here! Ten *kroner*, and here's another five. There you are, and good luck to you.'

'Oh, thanks, Dad.'

'Off you go, then. What are you waiting for?'

'Er . . . well . . . you see, now we've got our hand in . . .'

'Yes?'

'We could do your car now!' I completed Erik's sentence for him.

'Free!' offered Erik, generously.

'What? Where? When? Free! You bring tears to my eyes! Well, I'd be a fool to turn down an offer like that, wouldn't I? Do you do a good job?'

'You bet your life we do!'

Chapter 10

Next day we put one of the aerials in Specs's garden, among the pine trees, while Specs himself went to Hilleröd to buy the parts we needed. We had collected thirty-seven *kroner* altogether: thirty contributed by Erik and me and seven by Katya. She had earned four *kroner* helping the old lady in the villa called 'Belvedere' with her cleaning, and the rest was an advance on her pocket money.

When the aerial was up, we took the tools and electric cable and so on out to the hut to put up the other one. We'd picked a place for it the evening before, a spot where there were two enormous trees.

Specs joined us in the afternoon. He was lugging a bag crammed with all sorts of stuff. He was delighted with our aerial.

'That's perfect. I just have to do one or two things to the receiver at home now – but let's get everything ready here first. And we've got twelve *kroner* left! What shall we do with them?'

'Let's hide them here in the hut,' I suggested. 'We can keep them till we have something to celebrate, and then have a party.' The others agreed, and we put the money away underneath Specs's batteries. Then we watched him at work; there wasn't a lot the rest of us could do to help him Finally the equipment was ready, and all he had to do was connect up the earth, the batteries and the aerial. We crouched on the ground beside him, watching him closely.

'We were talking to Stoffer yesterday,' I said. 'He told us about your invention, Specs. It sounds great!'

'It's nothing special,' said Specs modestly. 'I haven't even tried it out properly yet, not in practice ... There, this ought to work now! This switch controls receiving and transmitting. Let's make sure the receiver's OK.'

He took off the ear-phones and handed them to me.

'That's a programme of records from Sweden you can hear,' he told me. 'I'd no idea it was so late! We'd better be getting home – it'll be supper time. I'll fix up the receiver in the garage after supper, and we should be able to begin transmitting about eight. How shall we divide up?'

'I'd like to be out here,' I said, and Katya said she would too.

We agreed to start transmitting at quarter past eight; Erik and Specs, back in the garage, were to have first go. Specs checked over the equipment at the hut with me again.

I got back to the hut rather early. About seven o'clock it had rained, but the sun came out again afterwards. The tree tops were wet from the rain and shining in the sun. I sat down and listened to the fishing boats chugging out into the little bay as I waited for Katya.

I'd brought along the alarm clock from my bedroom, so as to be sure of tuning in on time. I had also remembered to bring a notepad and pencil.

At last it was nearly quarter past eight, and I put the ear-phones on. The receiver was an old, rebuilt one, which could get quite a lot of different stations, and I didn't know yet just what wavelength Specs and Eric would be using.

Katya came running up, out of breath, and collapsed on the grass. 'Have they started?'

'Not yet.'

'Maybe their watches are slow.'

I moved the tuner slowly from side to side. All I got was the usual crackling noises, nothing else. I tried again. The alarm clock was standing on the transmitter, ticking loudly. Time passed slowly by.

'It's twenty-five past eight already!' said Katya.

I nodded. Something must have gone wrong. I tried the tuner again, very slowly this time.

'Let me try!'

'Ssh! Wait a minute!'

'Is that them?'

'I think so – quick, pass me my paper and pencil!'

Katya knelt down beside me and watched closely as I wrote the message down.

–.–. .– –. – I ––. . – I – .... .
I – .... .. –. ––. I – ––– I .––
––– .–. –.– I –.–. .– –. I –.––
––– ..– I .... . .– .–. I ..– ...
I –. ––– .–– I ... –.–

(Morse code, see page 127).

Then there was a loud crackle, and the transmitter was silent.

'What does "SK" mean?' asked Katya.

'It means their message is over, and now they're sitting by their receiver, waiting for us to transmit.' I turned the switch to the 'Send' position and connected up the aerial. Katya already had her finger on the sending key.

'What shall we say?'

'Say: Specs and Erik. Receiving you loud and clear.'

Katya began:

... .--. . -.-. ... I .- -. -.. I
. .-. .. -.-

When she had finished the message she too gave the 'SK' signal, and we switched back to 'Receive'. We heard them again at once. This time, they transmitted just one word, in Morse code:

--. .-. . .- -

Chapter 11

It was quite late by the time we finished. We telegraphed all sorts of things back and forth, and finally we fixed a time to meet next day.

It was a still night, and the patch of sky above the clearing was full of stars. Katya and I wandered slowly home through the wood.

'Do you remember the first day of the holidays, Kim?' Katya asked. 'When we were coming back from the station, and you and Erik were talking about Specs? You didn't seem to think much of him.'

'Or of you either!' I told her. 'At least, Erik didn't. We were used to being just the two of us, but personally I think it all turned out rather well. I like it the way we are now.'

'Specs's invention sounds very exciting.'

'Yes, doesn't it! I bet he'll be a professor one day, same as your father.'

'Maybe you're right. What do *you* want to be?'

'No idea! I've thought of being a lot of things in my time. When I was very little I wanted to be a road sweeper.'

'I mean, what would you like to be *now*?'

'And a bit later I wanted to join the fire brigade, and then I wanted to sell flowers, and be a milkman and a policeman and an airman and a taxi-driver and goodness knows what else.'

'And don't you want to do any of those things any more?'

'I really haven't thought about it much lately! Katya, do you think your father will get permission to stay in the country?'

'Oh, I do hope so, but it's not at all certain.'

'Why did he escape to Denmark? Politics?'

She shook her head. 'I don't know.'

'Politics are stupid,' I told her. 'Oh, look at that ship out there.'

We stopped to watch the ship. The noise of its engine carried across the water to us. It was a freighter, putting out to sea. I don't know how long we stood watching, but by the time we moved on again the ship was almost out of sight. All we could still see were its lights.

The moon came up out of the sea, big and red and round like an enormous blood orange, and very slowly rose higher. For a moment it looked as if it had glue on it and was going to stick to the water, or the water going to stick to it. But then they came unstuck; moon and sea were separate.

'It's lovely here,' said Katya quietly.

The wind had died down, and there was only a warm, gentle breeze blowing, as if someone or something were blowing warm air towards us from out to sea.

'Let's sit down for a moment,' Katya suggested.

She was carrying her jacket, so we spread it out on the beach and sat down on it. We stayed there for some time, without saying a word. Not because we couldn't think of anything to say; we just didn't feel like talking.

'I could do with a swim,' Katya said, breaking the silence.

'Me too,' I said.

'Shall we?'

'We haven't got our swimming things.'

'Does that matter?'

'I suppose not,' I admitted.

'I mean, do you feel shy of me or something?'

'N-no.'

'Coming in, then?'

'Right!'

I turned my back to her and got undressed; I didn't turn my back because of not wanting her to see me with nothing on, so much as because I thought it was the right thing to do. I tried not to look at her, either. Not that I wouldn't have liked to, but I was afraid she would be embarrassed or annoyed.

'Kim?'

I turned round. She'd taken her clothes off, and she didn't seem to be embarrassed, so I didn't need to be embarrassed either, which made things much simpler. Actually she looked very nice.

'Shall we run in?'

I took her hand, and we ran down to the sea together, over the wet, hard sand, and through the shallow water to the place where the bottom dips suddenly. I let go of Katya's hand as we met the first wave. She squealed when it broke over her, the way girls do. Then we swam side by side along the shore, slowly and comfortably, with long, leisurely strokes. The water was warmer than the air. Katya's hair got wet and tangled. It looked funny, and really quite pretty. We stayed in the water some time; it felt so good we couldn't bring ourselves to come out, and we kept swimming up and down the same bit of beach.

'Race you back!'

We swam back to shore. When the water got too shallow to swim we stood up and ran in. I could easily have been first, but I hung back slightly so that she could win, and thus get back to our pile of clothes first.

'I won!' she shouted, laughing.

'Here, you can use my shirt for a towel,' I said, tossing it towards her.

'Thanks.'

I dressed myself, and lit the pipe my uncle had recently given me; he said it was better for you than cigarettes. Then I sat down and waited for Katya.

We walked side by side the rest of the way home, hardly saying a word. I felt really good – better than I'd felt for ages, though I wasn't sure why. All of a sudden I felt I was walking on air.

I went as far as Moor House with Katya. There was a light shining in one window.

'Father's in his room, writing.'

'Good night, Katya,' I said. 'It was a nice evening.'

'It was, wasn't it? Good night.'

I set off for home. My aunt and uncle had gone to bed already. I took off my shoes, shook the sand out of them on the steps outside the house, and crept up to my room. I lay awake for some time, hands clasped behind my head, looking up at the ceiling. I felt very contented, and though I was dead tired I decided to stay awake a bit longer and enjoy the feeling. But all the same, I fell asleep quite soon afterwards.

Chapter 12

After Erik, Specs and I had gone on at our parents (or in my case my aunt and uncle) for a few days, we finally wore them down and got permission to sleep in the hut occasionally if the weather was fine. Katya had promised her father to go over his manuscript with him in the evenings – his Danish still wasn't very good – so we didn't have to feel bad about going to the hut and leaving her behind, though of course we'd have liked her company.

We each had a sleeping-bag, and we were going to put some old raincoats on the ground underneath them. We took tea and biscuits and Erik's banjo. The weather was perfect. When the sun set, we lit a camp fire outside the hut. The sky was still quite light, and when we'd had some tea and eaten almost all the biscuits, Specs and I began to smoke pipes.

As the fire burned low, we got around to talking about Spec's invention. He explained the whole thing in detail, though Erik and I didn't really understand much of it.

'Stoffer said you and he were planning to build your new type of carburettor into an actual car?'

'That's the idea, only we haven't got enough money to start on that yet.'

'How much would you need?'

'At least a thousand *kroner*.'

'It's not really all that much,' said Erik, looking thoughtful, just like Schnapp.

'No,' agreed Specs, 'not if you happen to have it! But if you need a thousand *kroner* and you don't have a single *ore*, then it's a lot of money!'

'Mm. Specs, suppose you do get the money, do you think Erik and Katya and I could help you with the work?' I asked.

'Would you really?'

'We'd love to!'

'Well, thanks,' said Specs. Then he sighed. 'If anything comes of it, that is – but where would we get that much money?'

'We'll have to put our minds to it,' said Erik, closing the subject. 'How about bed now?'

We spread the raincoats and sleeping-bags in a circle round the fireplace in the hut. Then we got into the bags, and lay there talking about this and that for a bit longer. Erik, who was next to the rebuilt radio set, switched it on and put on the ear-phones.

'Grandpa's going to listen to the radio,' he said jokingly. 'I'll tell you if there's anything really thrilling on Woman's Hour!'

'It's not Woman's Hour time now!' Specs told him. 'It's well past midnight – there won't be any Danish programmes being broadcast. You might find a foreign station.'

'That's what I'm trying to do. I've got a talk on a French station here – want me to translate?'

'Don't make me laugh! You know about as much French as Schnapp!'

'Believe it or not, Schnapp knows a lot! He can even ...' Suddenly we saw Erik listening intently.

'Hey! Wait a minute!' He picked up pencil and paper and began to write.

Specs and I sat up and looked over his shoulder.

–.– –.– –.– ... –.–

'There's someone transmitting from the

garage.' Erik said. 'A whole row of k's and then the end of message signal.'

We stared at each other. Specs said, 'Apart from you two, Katya's the only person who knows where I keep the key.'

'It must be Katya, then. Let's see what she wants.'

We switched over to 'Send' and began transmitting in Morse, using the same signal as she had done. Then we switched over again, and Erik put the ear-phones on and translated the letters out loud as Specs wrote them down in the notebook.

'T-w-o – m-e-n – a-r-e – l-u-r-k-i-n-g – i-n – o-u-r – g-a-r-d-e-n.'

We replied: 'C-o-m-i-n-g – a-t – o-n-c-e – w-a-i-t – t-h-e-r-e.'

Then we switched the set off and dressed at top speed.

'Crikey! This is the most exciting thing that's ever happened to me!' gasped Erik. 'Ready?'

'Yes. Come on, let's go. Bring the torch.'

We ran through the wood as fast as we could in the dark. When we reached the narrow path leading from the road to Moor

House, and past the Birks' bungalow, we slowed down to a walk.

There was no one to be seen; we crept closer, using the grass verge so as to muffle the sound of our footsteps. The garage door was closed, but when we tried the handle it opened. It was dark inside.

'Are you there?' we called to Katya.

'Yes,' she said. 'I didn't want to show a light. Thank goodness you've come! Those men are still there. I've just been down Specs's garden to see. They were standing in our garden whispering to each other. Father's in the house, writing. I didn't want to tell him – the doctor says he must have complete rest, and maybe it doesn't mean anything. Still, they've been prowling around the house for over half an hour now.'

'Come on,' I said briefly.

We all four crawled through the hedge and crossed the meadow. As soon as the two men heard us, they made for the path. When we turned and ran to cut them off, they quickened their pace.

'Hey – you there!' Erik shouted after them.

But the two men did not stop. They had reached the path now and were making for the road, fast.

'Shall we follow them?'

'No – let them go!'

'Well, we know now they were up to no good,' said Specs.

'I'm so thankful you came,' said Katya.

'Any idea what they were after?'

'Who could they have been?' wondered Erik. 'As far as I could make out, one of them was quite big, and the other was fat and much smaller. Like those two men we saw following your father the first day. But who are they?'

'There's a couple like that staying in the hotel on the front,' Specs remembered. 'Of course, that doesn't necessarily mean they *are* the same couple, but the description fits. I saw them the other day as I was passing the hotel. They were sitting in the garden having a meal.'

We heard a window being opened and a deep voice calling, 'Katya!'

'Coming!' she called back. Then she lowered her voice again. 'I'd better go in now. See you in the morning?'

'Why don't we all go swimming before lunch tomorrow, if it's fine enough?'

'Good idea,' said Katya. 'Goodnight, everyone – and thanks very much for coming round.'

'Good night.'

Specs, Erik and I went back to the wood, crawled into our sleeping bags again and lay awake a bit longer, discussing what had happened. At last we said good night and settled down to go to sleep. I was just dropping off when I felt an elbow in my ribs.

'You asleep?'

'No.'

'I was thinking. It's just like an adventure story. I mean, those peculiar men, and . . .'

'So what?' I asked. I was tired, and I wanted to get some sleep.

'What do you mean, so what? I was just thinking you ought to write it all down, Kim. Then we could give it to the others at school to read. They'll never believe us if we just *tell* them, but if you put it down on paper . . .'

'Mmph . . . maybe. Yes, it'd make a change.'

'That's right.'

'Mm. Perhaps I *will* have a go.'

'Great. Good night. Specs is asleep already.'

'Good night.'

I woke to find something dripping on my head, and when I opened my eyes I realized it was rain coming in through the smoke-hole in the roof of the hut. I sat up.

Erik and Specs were lying in funny, twisted positions, fast asleep. Specs had tossed and turned in his sleep so much that he was lying in quite a different place from the night before, with his head up against the fireplace. Erik had made a fearful mess of his sleeping bag, and his legs were now resting on the cold ashes of the fire.

Outside it was raining hard and steadily. Evidently this was not just a shower; it sounded as if the rain had really set in. I dug out a couple of biscuits and ate them. Specs and Erik were still snoring away. After watching them for a bit I decided I felt like talking to someone. They were not too pleased to be woken up.

'Oh, stop it, you twit!' groaned Specs.

'Let me sleep! What d'you want to go and wake me up for?'

'I'm not waking you up,' grunted Erik, still half asleep. '*You're* waking *me* up!'

'You pulled my nose.'

'I did not. *You* pulled *my* nose!'

'Shut up, both of you!' I said, laughing. 'I pulled *both* your noses. You've had quite enough sleep.'

'I have not!' yawned Specs.

'Oh, yes, you have. Come on, get up!'

'I think it's raining.'

'How right you are! It's fairly bucketing down.'

'I call it a shame!' grumbled Erik, sitting up and digging his fingers into his hair. 'A rotten shame, that's what I call it. Now what?'

'No idea. What do *you* think? Shall we stay out here or not?'

'A drop of rain won't hurt us. Have we got enough dry wood to make tea?'

'We haven't got any at all. We weren't expecting rain.'

'Why don't we go home now and come back when it clears up? We've slept here once now, anyway. Next time we must make sure we have dry wood and provisions.'

'I slept very well,' Specs announced.

'Me too. Well, how about going home, then? This rain looks as if it could go on all day, and I'm ravenous.'

Chapter 13

Not only did it rain all that day, but for the next two days as well. I didn't see much of the others during this time. It was very comfortable at my uncle's house. The rain poured down outside, and there was a high wind, but we were warm and cosy indoors, with big logs burning in the open fireplace all day.

I used these rainy days to do some writing, as Erik had suggested. I sat downstairs in the living room, by the fire, writing page after page about Erik and Katya and Specs and myself and our holidays, beginning with the first day of the holidays and going on till now, when things seemed to be getting quite exciting.

On the third day, when my aunt and uncle had gone to Helsingör to visit friends, Specs and Eric came bursting in.

I was sitting on our veranda, which is glassed in, writing, and Mr Rasmussen had settled down in an armchair and was deep in a book. It was still raining, but you could tell that the weather was soon going to improve. I let Specs and Erik in at the back door, and they took their boots off in the kitchen, so as not to leave muddy footmarks. We went up to my room. I could see Erik was in a state of great excitement.

'Has something happened?'

'I'll say it has! Just listen to this . . .'

'Hold on a moment and I'll get another chair.'

'Oh, never mind that! We can sit on the bed. Listen, I've tracked down the criminals!

'You mean those two men we saw the other night?'

'That's right. They really *were* the same two men Specs saw. You see, I was in the hotel on the front myself, with my Mum and Dad and a business friend of Dad's. We were going to have a meal there, and we'd hardly got into the restaurant when I spotted them. They were sitting at a table by the window, watching the rain. Then I brought off an absolute master-stroke – I worked it so that we were at the next table. And of course I made sure I had the best chair, so I was back to back with one of the men. I could hear every word they said!'

'So what *did* they say?'

'Nothing! I mean, nothing to start with. But when we got to the sweet course, the waiter came and called one of them to the telephone, and when he came back they started talking. I was listening so hard I quite forgot to eat!'

'Were they talking about Katya's father?'

'You bet your life they were! At least, I *think* they were talking about him. How did it go exactly? Yes . . . he said . . . hm, yes, now I remember. He said, "That was the boss. He thinks we'd better not spend any more time hanging about the place. Perhaps we should go down there at once?" The other man objected. "It's raining," he said. "Anyway, I think it would be better to wait till dark. Then we won't attract so much attention." Then the other one said, "You have a point there; they impressed that on me over the phone. We'll wait till evening, then. There's not all that much hurry – after all, he sits up writing half the night. Let's say midnight." There! What do you think of that?'

'What a bit of luck!' I cried. 'I can hardly believe it! What else did they say?'

'Not a lot. Oh, wait a minute – I forgot to tell you this too, Specs – the one who'd stayed in the restaurant asked, "What's the boss working on now?" And the other one said, "He's still tied up with those jewel robberies." What do you think of *that*? We've landed right in the middle of a bunch of real gangsters!'

'Well, I must say!' Specs was impressed. 'Listen – about tonight. We must work out a careful plan. If they have designs of some kind on Katya's father, we've got to stop them.'

'Perhaps we ought really to go to the police,' murmured Erik, without much enthusiasm.

'No, we can't,' I told them. 'You see, Katya's father doesn't have a passport and so on. If the police start looking at him too closely, he might be deported. We have to deal with this on our own.'

'Oh, well, if that's the way it is!' said Erik happily. 'Of course we can manage on our own! Pity we haven't got any pistols.'

'Well, we haven't, and that's that,' Specs interrupted. 'We have got rockets, though . . . I wonder if we could rig up something with them?

'How?' asked Erik doubtfully.

'Well, I was only thinking . . . is there any law that says you can't fire rockets anywhere except straight up in the sky? Of course we wouldn't aim any right *at* them – I don't think that would be very easy, anyway – but a few warning shots might do the trick.'

'Good idea!' I said. 'And I was wondering if we couldn't do something with that inductor thing of yours.'

'That's it – brilliant!' shouted Specs. 'Why didn't I think of it myself? Of course – we can pass an electric current through Katya's garden gate! It's made of wrought iron and set in cement! Couldn't be better! We'll electrify it, so they'll get a nasty shock if they try coming in. Look, I've got to go home for lunch now. When shall we meet?'

'Let's say eleven-thirty tonight, over at your garage.'

'Right! And we'd better not tell Katya, had we?'

'No – not a word. No need to frighten her. Crikey, this really *is* an adventure!'

'Eleven-thirty in my garage, then. I'll have everything ready. Coming, Erik?'

Specs and Erik ran downstairs together. The rain had stopped at last; it would be dry tonight.

Chapter 14

I lay awake in bed, staring at the ceiling. I was fully dressed, just waiting for my aunt and uncle to go to bed. I've never read a book where the hero had to think of silly little things like that when grappling with an international crime ring. However, I just had to put up with it; no doubt Erik and Specs were in the same position. I didn't feel at all like a hero, anyway. Not that I know how a hero *does* feel, but I doubt if his knees knock together like a pair of castanets, which is what mine were doing at the mere thought of what lay ahead.

In fact, the whole thing was really very strange. Here was I, lying in bed, an ordinary boy in an ordinary house in a remarkably ordinary seaside resort. Downstairs my uncle and aunt were moving about, and I could tell they were tidying the house and locking up for the night. Everything was the same as usual. Yet tonight things were going to happen that were right outside the events of an ordinary boy's experience.

It was a still night. I could hear the waves breaking on the beach and rolling back again. They sounded like long, deep breaths. Over in the wood, a cuckoo called. A car went past on the main road, its headlamps throwing their light on my bedspread; the beam of light crossed the room and vanished again.

I listened. The house was quiet now. My aunt and uncle must have gone to bed, and if I knew them, they'd be snoring already. Some other time I must write about the weird noises my uncle makes when he snores.

I waited another quarter of an hour, and then crept over to the window, very slowly and cautiously, because the floor is old, and the floorboards creak at the least thing.

Of course, I had to go and tread on the board that creaks worst of all! It positively screeched, and I stood quite still and waited, hardly daring to breathe. No sound from below. I sat on the window-sill, swung my legs over the edge, and wondered just where to jump. It had looked perfectly easy in, daylight, but in the dark I had trouble telling where my uncle's glass frames ended and his rosebed began. As I couldn't very well land on the glass frames, I'd decided to sacrifice a few roses. I knew they were my uncle's pride and joy, but there it was, I had no choice, did I? I mean, it wasn't as if I was jumping on his roses for fun!

The moon was in the sky, big and round, but of course, at the very moment I needed it, it had to go behind some enormous black clouds which were travelling at a snail's pace. However, I dared not wait till the moon came out again. I hung from the sill by my hands for a moment, then pushed myself off from the wall, and dropped.

Naturally I went and landed right on top of a rose bush, and not in a way I've ever seen any film star land when jumping off a wall. However, I disentangled myself from the thorns and crept across the lawn to the path.

I knocked the agreed signal on the garage door. The key turned cautiously in the lock, and the door opened.

'At last! I've been sitting here waiting for donkey's years. I'd almost given you up.'

'I couldn't get out of the house before. Erik should be along any moment.'

Specs was sitting on a packing case, his elbows on his knees, his hands folded under his chin, staring straight ahead.

'Everything ready?'

He nodded.

'The inductor's there on the table. The battery's in the black briefcase. I've got them connected up to each other already, so we only need connect them to the gate. The rockets are over there. I've trimmed the fuses down so they'll go off almost as soon as they're lit.'

'Won't that be dangerous?'

'Not if I do it. I shall duck to one side the moment I light them.'

'For goodness' sake be careful!'

'Don't worry, I will. How are you feeling? Are you frightened?'

'Yes!' I admitted.

'Good! So am I, but I thought I'd be the only one.'

'What about afterwards?' I asked.

'What do you mean, afterwards?'

'Well, I was wondering how it's all going to end. I can't somehow seem to imagine it.'

'Nor can I. I suppose we'll have to take it as it comes – play it by ear.'

'Hm, yes. I'm thinking of what we'll have to face tomorrow! I mean, what will they say about the rockets, and us going around in the middle of the night? And of course I had to go and squash my uncle's prize roses jumping out of the window.'

'Yes, I was thinking much the same sort of thing myself,' Specs admitted. 'Isn't it silly? This could be a matter of life and death, and here we sit feeling guilty about a few roses!'

Our conversation was interrupted by a knock on the door. Our signal. I turned down the light and opened the door.

'I couldn't get here any earlier. What a night!' Erik's eyes were shining.

'Don't shout so!' whispered Specs.

'What's the matter? Playing at funerals?'

'Pretty nearly,' I said.

Specs laughed. 'Oh, come on, let's go. Who wants to do what? I'm dealing with the rockets.'

'Wait a minute!' Erik protested. 'How about Kim and me?'

'You can see to that death-dealing gadget

Specs has on the table there,' I said. 'I'm going to lie in wait by the hedge.'

'Where do I hide with the inductor, then?' asked Erik.

'Behind the house. If they try to climb the fence there, you'll see them for yourself quite easily. If they attack the front of the house, which is what I suspect they'll do, I'll pull a string. You have one end of it, I have the other. When you feel me pull it, you switch on the current. Where *is* the string, Specs?'

'On the table.'

I picked it up and put it in my trouser pocket. 'Do me a favour – don't let your rockets off right at me!' I asked Specs.

'Well, if you find yourself in the line of fire, you must just throw yourself flat on the ground. Don't worry, though – I'm planning to aim diagonally upwards anyway, so they'll pass above everyone's heads. I don't actually want to hurt anyone.'

'I suppose not,' said Erik, slightly disappointed. 'Wouldn't you rather work the electrical stuff, Kim? Then *I* could keep watch in the front garden.'

'No, thanks very much!' I declined Erik's

offer. 'It was my idea, wasn't it? So I'm going to see a bit of action!'

'Oh, you are, are you?'

Specs intervened. 'Kim, don't you think it might be a good idea to take that big stick?'

'You do that!' said Erik, with enthusiasm. 'Knock their heads in!'

'Better be careful. They're sure to have revolvers.'

'Don't worry, I'll be careful all right.'

We put out the light and left the garage. I did take the stick with me, and I must say it was a comforting feeling to have it in my hand. We walked quietly over to Moor House, where we crawled through the hedge, and soon we had an electric current running through the garden gate. Specs was crouching on the house steps with his rockets. Erik and I squatted down beside him. There wasn't any point in going to take up action stations before we heard noises. The night was perfectly still, and two men couldn't possibly approach without making any sound at all, however careful they were. We waited there, motionless, our ears pricked. It was rather cool, and I was glad I'd brought my uncle's old raincoat, since I'd soon be having to lie down in the wet grass.

I was just about to whisper, 'I don't think they're coming at all,' when we heard steps, a long way off. The moon had gone behind another cloud. We sat still for a moment, hardly breathing, and then Erik and I got up very cautiously and crept off to our positions.

I lay down at the spot I'd chosen the day before, close to the hedge. From here, I could keep a watch on almost all of the front garden.

The men were coming closer. We heard them kick a pebble now and then, but otherwise they made very little noise. They were probably walking on the grass verge. My heart began to thud wildly.

And then, there they were. They stopped right outside the gate and had a brief, whispered conversation. I felt as though they must surely hear my heart beating. One of them put his hand on the latch of the gate, and I pulled my end of the string between me and Erik. A split second later the man swore.

'Careful!' he whispered to his companion.

'This gate's electrified.' Then his voice dropped to a whisper so quiet I couldn't make it out, however hard I tried. They were just too far off for me to hear what they were deciding to do. Then I saw one of them take off his jacket, and I realized that he was going to put it over the wrought iron gate to act as insulation. We hadn't thought of that! Well, we'd have to fall back on the rockets now.

The bigger of the two men approached the little gate again, this time protecting his hand with his jacket. I gave Erik the signal. He switched on the current, and the man pulled his hand back.

'What the . . .! The current's still coming through.'

'Your jacket's wet from the dew; I expect that's why,' replied the other man.

'You were the one who wanted to wait till tonight!'

'Damn it all, of course I did! This path's swarming with people in the daytime. If we're not to attract attention, then we must . . .'

'I don't know . . . I don't like this.'

'D'you think *I* like it?'

'Well, we've got to go through with it now. There's a hedge all round the garden; the gate is still the easiest way in. Let's try vaulting it.'

'He's sitting in there, writing.'

'He usually is.'

'Rather him than me!'

'We might be able to get over if we used my raincoat. Laid it across the gate and vaulted.'

'Let's see . . . yes, that's done the trick!'

'Right! Here goes.' The speaker put his hands on the raincoat over the gate, trying it out. I pulled on the string, but he still stood there with one hand on the coat. 'Yes, it's OK now,' he said.

'Fine. Go on, then, get a move on!'

'Give me a leg up, will you?'

This was the critical moment. If Specs failed us now . . .

But Specs did not fail us. Specs is the reliable sort. I don't know who got more of a fright, the two men or me. However, I had an advantage, because I was already lying on the ground. One of the men was actually astride the gate when the rockets shot past him with a loud bang. I've never seen anyone move so fast. You could see the shape of him for just a split second longer, and then he was gone without trace, as if the rockets had hit him and carried him away. The whole thing happened incredibly fast, much faster than I'm telling it here. For a brief moment, though it seemed to me to last for ever, everything was perfectly quiet. There was not a sound except the wind in the tree tops and the hoarse cry of a bird woken by the bang.

Then I made a discovery. Something that made my hair stand on end. There was something moving, only a little way away from me.

I realized what this meant at once. The man had thrown himself off the gate and *into* the garden – not, as I had thought, back on the other side. I pressed close to the ground, holding my breath. Without turning my head, I could see him crawling closer. I grasped the stick in both hands – it was the only weapon I had if he discovered me. My hands were trembling. I tried to keep them steady, but it was no good. Now he was past me, and I thought I was saved. And then the door of the house opened, very slowly, and a narrow beam of light fell into the garden. It opened further, and there was Katya in the bright light, small and thin in her striped pyjamas. The man put his hand in his hip pocket. I raised my stick and shot forward, brought the cudgel down, and the man whirled around like a top. The whole thing happened very fast, and before I knew what was happening I felt a sharp pain on my chin. After that, I don't remember any more.

Chapter 15

I was woken by the sound of voices. At first they seemed to be a long way off, then they came gradually closer, and I opened my eyes. I was lying in a strange room. It was dark all around me, with only the faint light of the clear summer night coming in through the window. I had a headache, and when I cautiously felt my chin it hurt badly. Then I remembered everything. I listened anxiously to the voices coming through the closed door. I knew two of them already; they belonged to the two mysterious men. The third voice was deeper, and I had difficulty understanding it. I came to the conclusion that it must belong to Katya's father. 'But why in the middle of the night?' he was saying.

'So as not to attract attention. Our orders were to keep it quiet.'

'And wonderfully well we succeeded, I must say!' put in the other. 'I imagine those damn rockets must have woken the whole neighbourhood!'

'But . . .' said Katya's father, obviously searching for words. 'But one might have thought that . . .'

'Well, you see, Professor, in the police we can't exactly . . .'

I don't know what else he said, because it was at this moment that light dawned on me, and I didn't listen to the rest. *Police!* What fools we'd been! In a moment I was by the window, moving as quietly as I could. The garden was not far below me. Cautiously, I pushed up the window and climbed out. Then I let myself drop. I stood still for a moment and listened. They were still talking up there; no one had heard me. I crept through the garden without a sound and ran back to my uncle's house.

It was a gloomy start to the day. I hadn't slept a wink all night. When it got light I stopped brooding, got out of bed, put on my dressing gown and sat down to go on writing where I'd left off.

When I had put down all last night's events on paper, I still sat there, looking out of the window and doodling mournful little figures on a bit of writing pad. It was stormy outside, the sky was dark and overclouded, and the wind was whipping through the trees in the garden. It looked like autumn, in July.

Then I heard the house coming to life down below. I put away my fountain pen and got dressed.

By the time I came down to breakfast my uncle had gone out. He was off to Hilleröd on business of some kind, and wouldn't be back till midday. I was not sorry. I didn't know just how I was going to break it to him that I'd done for a couple of his rose bushes in the night, and now at least I had a few hours' respite.

After breakfast I put on my windcheater and went down to the beach. At first I'd thought I'd go and see the others and discuss last night with them, but then I decided I'd rather go for a walk on my own. I didn't want to talk. In fact, I was in a very bad mood. Everything had seemed so right and obvious – and now I was cursing myself! Too much imagination, that was my trouble! What a fool I'd been! Of course, the others had been involved too, but there was no denying that I'd been the moving spirit!

What was more, I'd actually hit a policeman over the head with a stick. If the worst came to the worst, and there were magistrate's hearings and fines and trouble with parents, I'd have to face up to it. I'd been reading too many adventure stories, with schoolboys overpowering gangs of dangerous criminals with their bare hands and getting enormous rewards. But I'd never read a book where the young hero goes and hits a *policeman* over the head! That kind of thing only happens to you in real life.

A reward . . . to be honest, then, I had it all planned out. About the money, and how to spend it.

I'd had the best of intentions. I got the idea that time we were talking to Specs, and he was telling us about his invention. He needed money, and it occurred to me a little later that our two criminals might well be the answer to the problem. I was sure we had only to catch them to get the reward – I was quite convinced there must *be* a reward, of course. Well, there it is: sometimes I do a bit too much thinking.

So I had thought this was a good way of getting some money so that Specs and Stoffer could try out their invention. Once the idea crossed my mind I hadn't wasted too much time thinking about rewards – but I must admit I'd toyed with the notion now and then.

Oh, well, we certainly wouldn't be getting any reward for this! A stiff fine, more likely. One that would swallow up my pocket money for months to come.

I like walking on the beach in rough weather, when the air is full of salt and spray from the sea. The breakers had washed up wet, gleaming seaweed all along the beach. I walked against the wind; it did me good to feel the spray flying in my face.

Someone called me. Or rather, I *thought* I heard my name, because the breakers were very loud. But I didn't bother to look round and see if I was right. I didn't feel like talking to anyone.

However, there it was again, right behind me. So then I did turn round, and stopped. It was Katya.

'Hullo.'

'Hullo,' I replied, not very cheerfully.

'Where are you going?'

'Nowhere special.'

'Are you in a bad mood?'

'Not exactly. Just furious with myself.'

'What for?'

'For being so stupid. What actually did happen last night?'

'They said they'd knocked you out. But when we went into the room, you were gone.'

'I woke up and heard them talking, and I realized they were police. So I got out. What happened to the others?'

'Didn't you know? Just after the tall one hit you he shouted out, "Police!" And then Specs and Erik ran away.'

'Oh, I see. But then what? Did you carry me into the house? How about the fat one – the one I hit over the head?'

'Both of you were unconscious. First Father and the tall man carried the fat one into the house, and then you. The fat man was the first to come round. Then they both had a long talk with Father. Apparently that's what they'd come for. It seems they'd been shadowing him right from the start, ever since he first came into the country. And yesterday they were told to question him, but without making any fuss about it, because the police didn't want the newspapers finding out and writing pieces about it all. You see, Father's quite well known, and . . .'

'Yes, I see all that, but they didn't have to go slinking around the place at dead of night!'

'No, you're quite right! In fact, they said so themselves! They were very angry at first, but then they calmed down, and talked to Father, and had some beer and smoked some of his cigars. Of course, Father didn't have any papers he could show them, and he still doesn't speak Danish too well, so now we'll have to wait and see what happens. I do hope we'll get official permission to stay here.'

'A fine mess I made of things!' I muttered.

Katya walked beside me in silence for some time. Then she said: 'Kim, I want to say thank you for all you did . . .'

I gave her a wary look. I thought she must be laughing at me, but her face was perfectly serious.

'That's a funny idea – saying thank you for a thing like that!'

'It was very brave of you – all three of you.'

'Well, *I* wasn't brave,' I told her. 'I was scared to death the whole time.'

'And Father sent a message. He wants to say thank you too. He's going to invite you round to our house soon, and then we'll celebrate.'

'You must be joking! Isn't he furious with us?'

'Not in the least! He thinks it was very good of you to try and defend our house, and he didn't want to give the police your names. Actually, before they went, they and Father had really made friends. Look, I've got to get home again now, but I did want a word with you. Would you like to come part of the way with me?'

By the time I'd seen Katya home, and was on my own way back to my uncle's house, I was feeling a lot better. The only thing I still had on my mind was those roses. I hadn't confessed to knocking them about yet, and I didn't know just how I could manage to explain away the roses without having to tell the whole of the rest of the story too.

Chapter 16

I had been out longer than I thought. My uncle was back already, and the dining table was laid. It looked more festive than usual, with a bottle of Rhine wine in the middle, and a wine-glass at every place, and a large vase full of roses. I turned cold as I realized that they came from the rose-bed I'd trampled over last night.

'Time for lunch! Where've you been, boy?' asked my uncle. 'We were just going to start without you. Run upstairs quickly and clean yourself up.'

When I'd had a wash and combed my hair, I came down again to find them all in high good spirits, talking and laughing. I slid quietly into my place and took a slice of meat. 'Good gracious me, what a small helping!' said my aunt. 'You're not ill, are you, Kim?'

'No, I'm fine, thanks,' I said politely. 'Just not very hungry.'

I couldn't help wondering all the time

when my uncle was going to ask about the roses. Not that he looked angry – quite the opposite. Picking up the wine bottle, he said, 'Like a drop of this, Kim? Kindly donated by Mr Rasmussen, who felt we should have a little celebration.'

'Well, I had to atone for my clumsiness this morning! I still feel bad about that.' Mr Rasmussen turned to me. 'I went and fell right into your uncle's rose-bed this morning, Kim! Just stumbled into it.'

'Oh, please don't mention it any more!' my aunt begged him. 'We're just glad you didn't hurt yourself.'

'That's right – what are a few roses?' agreed my uncle. 'Neither here nor there! I'd have had to cut them soon anyway. As it is, they come in useful as a flower arrangement.'

I sat there absolutely rigid, forgetting to eat. There they were, chatting about the roses I'd ruined last night, and acting as if it wasn't so bad after all and Mr Rasmussen had done it! I thought it was fantastically noble of him to take the blame; the only thing was, I couldn't explain to myself *why* he was doing it. I glanced at him, and he smiled back, and when no one else was watching he winked at me. All of a sudden I discovered how hungry I was, and I pretty soon set my aunt's fears about my health at rest.

It rained that afternoon. I was sitting on the veranda reading *The Three Musketeers* when Mr Rasmussen came out and joined me.

'Ah, here you are, young man!'

'Yes,' I said. 'Mr Rasmussen, I want to say thank you. About the roses. It was very nice of you.'

'Don't mention it. There's something I want to discuss with you, Kim.' He sat down beside me. 'The fact is, I've got something on my conscience. You see, a few days ago I did something that one really ought not to do . . . well, do you remember the day you were sitting out here writing something, not so long ago? Good. Then, if I remember correctly, your two friends came round, and you all three went up to your room. You left your papers down here, and I must confess, I couldn't help myself – I read some of it. Do you mind very much?'

'Goodness, no!' I said. 'Not in the least. It's just something I was writing about our holidays.'

'Well, today, when you were out for your walk, I went up to your room to see if you'd written any more. You see, I really wanted to know what happened next! What are you planning to do with your story, Kim?'

'Oh, nothing, really. I only wrote it down for fun, sort of . . . Erik gave me the idea.'

'May I borrow it for a few days? I'd like to send it to a friend of mine.'

'Of course you can.'

Then my uncle came down, and they started talking about something else.

Chapter 17

Four days later I went out to the hut. Specs and Stoffer had gone to Copenhagen together, and we didn't expect them back for a week. Erik and Katya would be at the hut by now. I had asked them to be there this evening, but I didn't tell them why.

I was carrying a big bag which belonged to my aunt, and when I thought of all the things inside it I felt even more pleased with life than I was already. I think I laughed out loud now and then as I went along, and the people I met must have thought I had a screw loose. But I didn't mind about that.

When I reached the clearing and our hut, Erik came to the door. 'Kim!' he called out. 'Thank goodness you're here at last! Someone's pinched our money.'

'Don't worry,' I laughed. 'That was me. I took it.'

'*You?*' said Katya, coming out of the hut.

'That's right, me. We're celebrating this evening.'

'But . . .'

'I'll tell you all about it in a minute. Help me get this lot unpacked first, will you?'

I opened the bag and sat down on the grass, while the other two unpacked it.

'A whole bottle of orange – great!' said Erik, smacking his lips.

'And a packet of biscuits.'

'Tea.'

'Three bars of chocolate – that's one each.'

'There are chocolate chips, too – in that pink bag,' I said.

'What's in this?'

'You needn't unpack that. It's just glasses and straws, for the orange. Watch out, those are strawberries. A whole kilo!'

'Cake, too. How many slices?'

'Twelve,' I said. 'Four each.'

'And two large candles. Great! Super-great!'

'But what's up?' asked Katya. 'Why are we celebrating this evening? Has something nice happened?'

'I'll say it has!'

'Yes, but what?' asked Erik. 'Have you won a prize in the lottery?'

'Even better.'

'Oh, come on, tell us!' cried Katya impatiently. 'Don't keep us in suspense.'

I let them go on asking for a bit; I wanted to put off the pleasure of telling them for a little longer.

'All right, then, listen!' I said at last. 'We agreed to save those twelve *kroner* for a day when something specially good happened – something that we'd want to celebrate.'

'Carry on!'

I put my hand in my pocket.

'Well, I thought that time had come! Look at this! Catch!' And I threw what I had in my hand in the air. A whole lot of hundred *kroner* notes fluttered up and then drifted to the ground.

Erik jumped up, his eyes popping. Katya couldn't speak; she sat there with her mouth open, looking at the notes.

'Is that *your* money?' cried Erik.

'It's all of ours,' I explained.

'You're nuts! You must be! Those are hundred *kroner* notes - how many are there?'

'Ten.'

'But . . . but . . . how . . . where did you get them?'

'I earned them.'

'What for? Kim, if you don't tell us the whole story, right from the beginning . . .'

'That's just what I was going to do, only you will keep interrupting. It was really all your idea, Erik.'

'*My idea?*'

'That's right. You remember the night we slept in the hut?'

'Of course I do. What about it?'

'That was when you suggested I should write things down about our holidays.'

'Yes, I remember that.'

'Well, there you are. That's what I did, when it was so wet outside. You know that a friend of my uncle's has been staying with us for the last few days?'

'Yes. Mr Rasmussen.'

'Well, the day you and Specs came to see me, he read what I'd been writing. And four days ago he asked me to lend him my story for a few days. He said he wanted to send it to a friend in Copenhagen. Of course, I thought he was nuts, but I let him have it.'

'And then what?'

'He sent it to his firm. He's a publisher. He asked them if they thought they could use it.'

'Use it? What for? You mean, in a book?'

'Yes. And today . . .'

'But . . . do you mean you're . . . good grief, this is like a fairy tale or something!' Erik did a wild war dance, beaming all over his face.

'So they *can* use it?' asked Katya.

'Looks like it. They want to take a bit out here and there, and alter a few things, but apart from that . . . And the best thing is that they sent a cheque at the same time as the letter! I went straight off to Hilleröd and got it cashed. I thought we ought to use the money for Specs's invention.'

'But it's really *your* money. It was you that . . .'

'Nonsense!' I interrupted Erik. 'I'd never have had anything to write about, if you others hadn't been around. Shall we use the money for Specs's invention, then?'

'Of course! OK, Katya? I say, what a thing! Why did you cash the cheque, Kim?'

'I wanted just to see all that money, all at once.'

'Good idea. Fancy actually holding a bundle of hundred *kroner* notes like that! Want to try it, Katya?'

He passed Katya the money, and she held it reverently for a few moments, then passed it back to me, and I passed it on to Erik again. We were so happy we acted as if we were quite crazy.

It was dark by now. We put the money in an old tin, and buried it in the wood by moonlight, forming a solemn circle around the hiding place and watching as Erik filled in the little hole again.

'I can't wait to see Specs's face when we dig it up!' said Katya.

'I never thought we'd have a chance to dig up real buried treasure!' I murmured. 'Well, these are certainly the most exciting holidays I've ever had!'

'Dead right!' Erik agreed.

Morse Code

Letter	*Signal*
A	.–
B	–...
C	–.–.
D	–
E	.
F	..–.
G	––.
H	....
I	..
J	.–––
K	–.–
L	–..
M	––
N	–.
O	–––
P	.––.
Q	––.–
R	.–.
S	...
T	–
U	..–
V	...–
W	.––
X	–..–
Y	–.––
Z	–– .